JUL   1995

NATIVE AMERICAN LEADERS
OF THE WILD WEST

QUANAH PARKER

❖Comanche Warrior❖

William R. Sanford

ENSLOW PUBLISHERS, INC.

Bloy St. & Ramsey Ave.	P.O. Box 38
Box 777	Aldershot
Hillside, N.J. 07205	Hants GU12 6BP
U.S.A.	U.K.

Library of Congress Cataloging-in-Publication Data

Sanford, William R. (William Reynolds), 1927–
    Quanah Parker: Comanche warrior / William R. Sanford.
        p.   cm. — (Native American leaders of the Wild West)
    Includes bibliographical references and index.
    ISBN 0-89490-512-0
    1. Parker, Quanah, 1845?–1911—Juvenile literature. 2. Comanche
Indians—Biography—Juvenile literature. 3. Comanche Indians—Kings
and rulers—Juvenile literature. 4. Comanche Indians—History—
Juvenile literature. I. Title. II. Series: Sanford, William R.
(William Reynolds), 1927– . Native American leaders of the Wild
West.
E99.C85P387 1994
973'.04974'0092—dc20
    [B]   93-42258
                                                              CIP
                                                              AC

Printed in the United States of America

10 9 8 7 6 5 4 3 2 1

Photo Credits: Fort Sill Museum, pp. 12, 13, 17, 20, 23, 24, 27, 29, 31, 36, 40,
41; National Archives, pp. 34, 39; William R. Sanford, pp. 6, 15, 21, 35;
Smithsonian Institution, p. 8.

Cover Illustration: Paul Daly

══CONTENTS══

AUTHOR'S NOTE

This book tells the true story of the Comanche chief, Quanah Parker. Many mistakenly believe that his fame rests on one battle, Adobe Walls. His true fame, however, comes from his success in two roles, those of warrior and statesman. Among white settlers, his name evoked fear. For a decade, his raids in Texas brought death and destruction. After his surrender, though, he led the Comanche in making the hard adjustment to the white man's road. During his lifetime, stories about Quanah Parker filled the press. Some were fiction, but others were true. The events described in this book all really happened.

During his years of raiding, Quanah was both feared and hated. In his later years, he was admired and liked by the whites with whom he dealt. Only one Native American chief succeeded well in both worlds. His name was Quanah Parker.

QUANAH FIGHTS AT ADOBE WALLS

The United States Army's top general was William T. Sherman. He believed there was only one way to end the fighting with the Native Americans. Kill all the buffalo and that would wipe out their source of food and clothing. It was "the only way to bring lasting peace and allow civilization to advance."[1] Soon, buffalo hunters were killing buffalo by the million. Some freight trains from the West carried only buffalo skins. The hides sold for three dollars apiece.

On the southern Great Plains, white hunters were killing the buffalo in great numbers. Soon the Comanche would find none at all to hunt. Isatai was a medicine man in Quanah Parker's band of Comanche. It was his idea to wage war against the buffalo hunters. He said his magic would protect them in battle. "Those white men can't shoot you," he promised. "With my medicine, I will stop

White buffalo hunters killed off the greater part of the herds on the Great Plains by the end of the 1880s.

all their guns. . . . You will wipe them all out."[2] Then the buffalo would return. The tribes could resume their old ways of life. Quanah believed in Isatai's powers. In the spring of 1874, Quanah led the Comanche in a Sun Dance for the first time. This ceremony would insure their victory. Kiowas, Arapahoes, and Cheyenne came to join Quanah's group. He would lead them on a raid against the buffalo hunters.

Raiding was a way of life for the Comanche. Warfare

between tribes had always given warriors a chance to prove their bravery. Now the buffalo hunters and the white settlers were the other tribes.

Quanah learned that a band of white hunters was at Adobe Walls. This trading post lay on the Canadian River in north Texas. Ten years earlier, Kit Carson had attacked the Comanche there. On June 27, 1874, Quanah led seven hundred warriors toward the hunters' camp. He told them they would find the hunters asleep in the predawn dark. Meanwhile Isatai had painted himself yellow to honor the sun. He rode up to the top of a nearby hill to watch his prophecies come true.

The twenty-eight hunters (and one woman) were not asleep. About two o'clock that morning, a loud bang had awoken them. A ridgepole in one building had snapped. The hunters worked to fix it before the roof fell in. One hunter, Billy Dixon, spotted the horses of Quanah's men. As he watched, the warriors spread out and attacked. They gave a single long war whoop. Dixon saw that this was not a raid to steal horses. The warriors were heading straight for the camp. Quickly the hunters barred the doors of the three buildings they occupied.

Isatai had promised the warriors that they could kill the sleeping whites with clubs. Quanah led his warriors right up to the buildings. The attackers tried to smash their way in with gun butts and clubs. Quanah climbed atop one building. He tried to punch holes in the sod roof and set the building afire. Fire from the hunters' heavy

The Comanche leader, Quanah Parker, led his people for many decades.

rifles drove him off. The warriors retreated, then charged again. Each time the hunters drove them back. Once, a bullet killed Quanah's horse. As Quanah hit the ground, a bullet creased his shoulder. A mounted rider dashed up to his rescue.

The attacks lasted until noon. Then Quanah called his men back. Fifteen warriors lay dead. Many more had wounds. Isatai made an excuse. He said the attack failed because someone in the party had broken a taboo. Quanah knew better. One Comanche summed it up, "The buffalo hunters . . . had telescopes on their guns. Sometimes we would be standing way off, resting and hardly thinking of the fight. They would kill our horses."[3] One shot became famous. Billy Dixon killed a rider with a single shot. Later he measured the distance. It was 4,614 feet.

After Quanah broke off the attack, he led his force back onto the Staked Plains. That summer, Comanche raiders attacked from Texas to Colorado.

CYNTHIA ANN PARKER
BECOMES A COMANCHE

In 1834, the Parker family moved to Texas from Illinois. They settled on the bottomlands of the Brazos River. There they built a log stockade. Other frontier families joined them. These thirty or so pioneers made up the westernmost white settlement in Texas.

On May 19, 1836, many of the men had left Parker's "fort" to work in the fields. Without warning, a hundred mounted warriors appeared outside the wall. Most of them were Comanche. One waved a soiled white flag. John Parker, leader of the settlers, sent his son Benjamin to talk with them. The band asked for beef to eat. When Benjamin refused, they killed him with lances. The horsemen dashed into the fort. They killed the adults, but Lucy Parker and her four small children slipped away. They headed for the river. Warriors briefly captured all five, but a man from the fort attacked the warriors. He forced the warriors to drop Lucy and two of the children. The warriors rode off with Cynthia Ann Parker, aged nine, and John Parker, aged six.

The war party rode their horses hard until midnight. At last, they stopped to make camp. Then they held a victory dance. The raid had been a triumph. No one had been killed or wounded. The captives were proof of their success. At dawn the dance broke up. The Comanche took the Parker children west. Cynthia and John survived the shock of capture. The Comanche adopted them into the tribe. Soon the children spoke the language and dressed like other Comanche.

Cynthia Ann Parker took the Comanche name Naduah. Once an army officer saw her at a council. She refused to speak in English. There was no sign that she was unhappy. She seemed to remember little of her early life. Around 1845, she married the warrior Peta Nokona. The couple had three children. Quanah, the oldest, was born around 1847.[1] His name meant Fragrant. Quanah's brother, Pecos (Peanut), was two years younger. His sister Topsannah (Flower) arrived a few years later.

The sun on the Plains tanned Naduah's skin. Soon, except for her blue eyes, she looked like other Comanche women. Quanah's mother carried out the many tasks of a wife. She made the family's clothing, bedding, tools, and tipi cover. When the band moved, she packed and unpacked all their belongings. Often she left the camp to gather wild fruit and other plants. Fruit came from the

Cynthia Ann Parker, the daughter of white settlers, was the mother of Quanah Parker.

prickly pear cactus and persimmon and plum trees. Other trees provided acorns and piñon and hickory nuts.

Naduah spent much time preparing their meals. The family diet included dried meat, game, fruits, vegetables, and herbs. Quanah's father hunted, killed, and butchered the game. Buffalo meat was the most common. The band also ate deer, antelope, and elk. Naduah stewed the meat in metal pots. She flavored it with wild onions and roots. Whenever he was hungry, Quanah could dip into the rich broth and pick out a tasty chunk.

Naduah made Quanah's clothes from buckskin. He wore a loose-fitting shirt, leggings, and moccasins. A breechcloth was tucked into a belt in front and back. In cold or wet weather, Quanah slept in the family tipi. Ten to twenty buffalo hides made up the tipi's cover. The hides rested on a framework of four large and a dozen smaller poles. During hot months, Quanah slept under a brush shelter, which was open to cooling breezes.

For Quanah, growing up was a time of waiting and training. He soon would become a Comanche warrior.

The Comanche made shelters of brush and small trees for shade on the Staked Plains.

QUANAH BECOMES
A WARRIOR

Quanah lived in the Comanchería. Most of this area lay in what is now Texas and western Oklahoma. It also took in parts of Kansas, New Mexico, and Colorado. The Comanche had not always lived on these southern plains. In the early 1600s, the Comanche lived in the mountains of Wyoming and Montana. They were a Shoshonean people. They moved south to hunt buffalo on the plains.

The Utes told the Spanish in New Mexico about the Comanche. They called them *Koh-Mahts*, or strangers. The Spanish wrote this as *Kamantcia*. In English, this became *Comanche*.[1] A total of 20,000 Comanche lived in five main groups. The southernmost group lived in central Texas. Their name, *Penateka*, meant Honey Eaters. Where they lived, there were many trees from which they gathered wild honey. The *Nokoni* (Wanderers) roamed Texas close to the Red River. In Oklahoma, the *Kotsoteka*

(Buffalo Eaters) hunted the great herds of buffalo there. The *Yamparika* (Root Eaters) lived in what is now southern Kansas. When he was an adult, Quanah led the *Quahadi* (Antelope) group. They lived on the Staked Plains. These vast grasslands are now in northwest Texas and eastern New Mexico.[2]

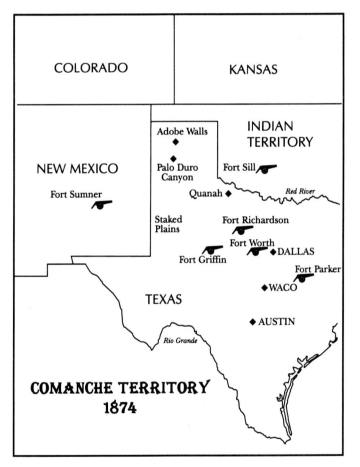

The territory of the Comanche included Texas, New Mexico and the Indian Territory (now Oklahoma). This region became a central area for cattle ranching, and settlers wanted to push the Comanche out.

No one chief led all the Comanche. Each group had its own council, peace chiefs, and war chiefs. All adult males in a band made up the council. All could speak. Decisions had to be unanimous. If everyone did not agree, the Comanche postponed the matter. The peace chief was often one of the oldest men in the band. He could not order; he could only advise or suggest. If the group decided on war, the war chief could give orders. His power lasted only as long as the raid, though. Quanah's father, Peta Nokona, was a subchief. He led a small band of Nokoni warriors.

Quanah's training began as soon as he could ride a pony. His father owned hundreds of horses to choose from. At first, Quanah rode with an adult holding him. Soon he could ride alone. He began to practice with the bow and arrow. As the horse was galloping, he would drop to the side of his horse. This would screen him from an enemy's fire. Quanah learned to shoot his arrows while leaning under the neck of his horse.[3]

When he was a teenager, Quanah went on a vision quest. He left camp carrying only a robe, pipe, tobacco, and flint. He washed at a spring, then sat on the robe to fast and pray. After three days, he had seen no signs from the Great Spirit. But, on the fourth day, he saw an eagle above him. It dove to the ground, landing on a snake. As it flew off, the eagle lost one of its feathers. Quanah heard a voice telling him the quest was over. He picked up the feather and two stones that the snake had lain on. He

Quanah Parker led the Comanche in raids that involved travel on horseback for hundreds of miles.

placed them in a leather bag. This was the start of his medicine bundle, the power that was given to each warrior.

In 1859, Quanah and his father went off on a buffalo hunt. A force of Texans led by Sul Ross attacked the Nokoni camp. The raiders captured Quanah's mother and his baby sister. They saw that she was a white woman and took her with them. Cynthia Ann Parker grieved for her husband. She and her baby both soon died. Some say she died of grief. In 1861, Quanah's father led a raid against the Apaches. He died of wounds received in that battle.

The now-orphaned Quanah went to live with other bands. He spent a year with the Kotsoteka. In 1862, the Quahadi chief, Yellow Bear, invited Quanah to join his band.

QUANAH BEGINS
MARRIED LIFE

During the Civil War (1861–1865), 60,000 white men left Texas to fight in that war. The Comanche continued their war against the whites who had intruded into their homeland. They raided and burned their way through central Texas. The raiders followed a pattern. First they set up camp near their target. They left a change of horses there. Then they swooped in for the attack. Coming back to the camp, they rode on rocky ground to hide their trail. It took hours for the settlers to round up a relief force. By then the raiders, now on fresh horses, were miles away. They rode up to a hundred miles without stopping for rest or food. The Comanche killed hundreds of settlers. Farms and ranches turned into piles of charred ruins. After the war, an army officer said, "This rich and beautiful section does not contain as many white people as it did when I visited it 18 years ago."[1]

Quanah fell in love with Weckeah, Chief Yellow Bear's daughter. He was jealous when Tannap courted her. Tannap's father offered Yellow Bear ten horses if Weckeah would marry Tannap. Quanah had only four horses. Friends offered to lend him a dozen more. Tannap's father heard of the plan. He raised his offer to twenty horses. Yellow Bear was amazed. He had thought ten horses was a high price. He said Tannap could claim his bride in three days.

Quanah's friends made a plan. Quanah would elope with Weckeah. The young warriors would go with them and start a new band. The lovers and the warriors stole from the camp. They rode all night. The next day, they split up. Each group went in a different direction. Yellow Bear did not know which trail to follow. The band met days later miles away.

Quanah led his warriors on raids in west Texas. His band took many horses. Other warriors and their wives joined them. Within a year, Quanah led a band numbering 200 warriors.

The Comancheros were traders from New Mexico. They traded guns and supplies for horses. Texans hated the Comancheros. The traders provided the weapons the Comanche used to kill Texans. The Comancheros used to have trade fairs. Yellow Bear caught up with Quanah in the spring of 1867 at one of these trade fairs. Before fighting broke out, tribal elders proposed a truce. Neither side could afford to lose warriors. Quanah paid Yellow

Quanah, shown here with three wives, refused to choose one and drive off the others.

Bear and Tannap many horses. After being on their own for a year, Quanah's band rejoined the Quahadi.

That summer Quanah was ill with high fevers. In the fall he was too weak to hunt or raid. He decided to visit the peace council at Medicine Lodge Creek in Kansas. The United States Congress had set up a commission to make peace with the Plains tribes. Quanah met Philip McCusker there. McCusker told him of the death of Quanah's mother. For the first time, Quanah learned his mother's surname. From then on, he called himself Quanah Parker.

The leaders of many Comanche bands signed the Medicine Lodge Treaty. They promised to stop attacking whites. They would go onto a reservation. In return they would receive goods, tools, and equipment for thirty years. Toshaway, a Yamparika leader, issued a warning.

He said, "I shall wait until next spring to see if these things will be given to us. If they are not, I and my young men will return to our wild brothers to live on the prairie."[2]

The whites made a mistake. They thought the Comanche leaders could speak for all their bands. No Quahadi had signed the treaty, so Quanah's band was not bound by the treaty. He increased his attacks on the settlers. The other bands did not receive the promised goods. They too started raiding in Texas again. A party of 150 Comanche attacked a wagon train in May 1871. They tortured and murdered most of the teamsters driving in it. One man escaped. He made his way to Fort Richardson, headquarters of General Philip Sheridan. Sheridan ordered Colonel Ranald Mackenzie to put a stop to Comanche raiding.

Hunters traveled by train. They killed large numbers of buffalo whenever they met a herd.

A NEW FOE ON THE STAKED PLAINS

To the Comanche, the Staked Plains had always been a safe haven. This began to change in 1871. Colonel Mackenzie led a group of black soldiers, known as "buffalo soldiers." They formed the tough Fourth Cavalry. Their base, Fort Richardson, Texas, lay northwest of Dallas.

When the Fourth rode out on August 2, they went to hunt Quanah Parker. For six weeks, the soldiers found burned ranches and fresh graves. They found no trace of Quanah. As always, the Comanche struck, then retreated onto the Staked Plains. Mackenzie retreated back to his base. He knew he would have to lead his men onto the Staked Plains. Only then could he find and defeat Quanah.

Mackenzie gathered his forces once more. In late September the 600 soldiers were getting ready to move out again. Only twenty miles away from their camp, the Comanche raided a ranch. They stole a dozen horses and 120 cattle. Two nights later, the thunder of hoofs awoke the soldiers. Buffalo pounded into their camp. Mackenzie knew the Comanche had caused the stampede.

The soldiers headed for one of Quanah's known campsites, Canyon Blanco. That night Quanah led an attack on the soldiers' camp. His warriors dragged buffalo hides behind their horses to scatter the campfires of the soldiers. They fired, yelled, and rang cowbells. Quanah led half a dozen warriors straight to the Army horses. The horses fled in a wild stampede. The raid gained over 70 horses for the Comanche. Among them was Mackenzie's gray pacer.

General Ranald S. Mackenzie led the army in campaigns against the Comanche.

Another time, Lieutenant Robert Carter led a group of soldiers out to look for missing horses. Quanah led the attack on them. Carter wrote:

> A large and powerfully built chief led the bunch on a coal-black racing pony. . . . With six-shooter poised in air, he seemed the incarnation of savage . . . joy. His face was smeared with war paint. . . . A large, cruel mouth added to his ferocious appearance. A full-length head-dress . . . of eagle's feathers [spread] out as he rode. . . . Large brass hoops were in his ears. He was naked to the waist. . . . A necklace of bear's claws hung about his neck. His scalp lock was carefully braided and tied with bright red flannel. . . . Bells jingled as he rode at headlong speed.[1]

Quanah Parker, in war bonnet and leather jacket, was an awesome force on the southern Great Plains.

Quanah broke off the attack when a relief party arrived. The soldiers then chased the fleeing Comanche. For the first time, the army moved onto the Staked Plains. An early blizzard forced Mackenzie to turn back. The campaign was over for the year.

Mackenzie returned to the Staked Plains the next year. He led his men into land they had never seen before. They always seemed to be a day or two behind Quanah. The troopers crossed Texas into New Mexico before turning back. By mid-August they were back at Canyon Blanco. They had crossed the Staked Plains by two routes. The region was a mystery no more. In September, the army attacked a camp of the Kotsoteka (Buffalo Eaters). They killed 52 warriors and 130 women. Three thousand horses fell into army hands.

Quanah camped nearby. That night Quanah attacked the army camp. His warriors took back the Comanche ponies. They took some Army mounts as well. The army returned to Fort Richardson. Mackenzie had lost another campaign against Quanah Parker.

MACKENZIE CONQUERS
THE STAKED PLAINS

Quanah's attack on Adobe Walls the next year angered General Sherman. He sent a plan to President Ulysses S. Grant. The United States Army would give the Native Americans on the Plains a deadline. All who were not on a reservation by August 4, 1874, would be attacked. General Miles' Fifth Infantry would come onto the Staked Plains from the north. Major Price would lead the Eighth Cavalry from the west. Colonel Davidson's Tenth Cavalry would move in from the east. Colonel Ranald Mackenzie's Fourth Cavalry would complete the circle. They would move onto the Staked Plains from the south.[1] The army would keep the tribes on the run. They would become exhausted and surrender. Grant approved the plan.

Mackenzie arrived at the Staked Plains on September 23. Twice the Comanche attacked at night. They were trying to stampede the cavalry horses. Each time the troopers drove them off. The soldiers captured a Comanchero, José Tafoya. Mackenzie knew that Tafoya could tell him where Quanah was camping for the winter. Tafoya would not talk. The troopers rolled up a wagon. They raised a wagon tongue upright. They said that if Tafoya did not talk, they would hang him. The bluff worked. Tafoya promised to lead Mackenzie to Quanah's

This circa 1880 photograph shows Quanah in full war costume.

hidden camp in Palo Duro canyon. The troopers did not even know that this canyon existed.

Late on September 27, Mackenzie led his troops near Tule Canyon. He knew Comanche scouts watched his movements. As soon as it was dark, he changed routes. He followed Tafoya's route to Palo Duro Canyon. His men rode all night. At dawn they peered down into the secret canyon. A clear stream ran along the bottom. Lodges stretched beside it for three miles, 200 in all. The Comanche were still asleep. Here, in this remote stronghold, they felt safe.

The one trail into the canyon was steep and narrow. It ran a thousand feet down the cliffs. Mackenzie ordered his troopers to dismount. They led their horses down the trail. In single file, they would be easy targets. Three companies reached the bottom. Only then did a sentry fire a warning shot.

One company of troopers reached the Comanche herds. They cut them loose. Quanah's men would have to fight on foot. They missed Quanah's leadership. He was not there at the time. The warriors fought from behind rocks. Behind them, the women and children fled upstream, leaving the canyon. The campsite became littered with robes, cooking pots, clothing, and blankets. Two thousand horses galloped back and forth wildly. The thunder of their hooves rose above the noise of battle. The smoke of burning tipis filled the air. One frightened trooper yelled, "How will we ever get out of here?"

Quanah married many times. Here he is shown with Tonacey, his seventh wife.

Mackenzie remained calm. "I brought you in," he said, "and I will bring you out."[2]

The Comanche found their way out of the canyon in small groups. Mackenzie did not try to pursue them. His men were weary. They had covered twenty-five miles in only a few hours, then fought in fierce combat. The battle was not a bloody one. Only a few troopers received wounds. Four Comanche lay dead. But it was still a major victory. A cold, brutal winter would come early that year. Quanah's band would find it hard indeed to survive the coming months.

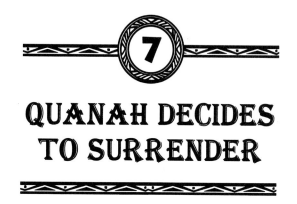

QUANAH DECIDES TO SURRENDER

Quanah's camp had held the supplies his band needed to last the winter. There were tons of flour, sugar, and cured meat. Soldiers found crates of new carbine rifles and bullets. Mackenzie acted quickly. He ordered everything burned. Far out on the prairie, Quanah could see the black smoke arising from the bonfire. Mackenzie knew that Quanah's men would try to steal back their horses. He allowed his scouts to load some with the loot they had taken from the Comanche camp. He ordered the more than a thousand others shot. Their bones lay there for many years. A trader finally hauled them away for sale as fertilizer.[1]

After the defeat at Palo Duro canyon, Quanah led his band south. They headed toward warmer weather in Mexico. Without horses, it was hard to hunt large game. They lived on nuts, roots, and rodents. Soon they began to raid Mexican ranches. Within months they had 2,000 horses. Quanah hoped to return to Palo Duro to hunt buffalo in the spring of 1875.

In April of 1875 three Comanche brought a message from Mackenzie. All the other bands had given up. They were on the reservation near Fort Sill. Troops still patrolled the Staked Plains. No place there would be safe for Quanah's band. Mackenzie's message was simple. If Quanah led his band in at once, they would not be punished. If he did not, Mackenzie would wipe them out. He would offer no mercy.

Quanah went to a small hill to pray. He asked the Great Spirit for a sign. He saw an eagle circling above. It swooped down and snatched up a snake. As he watched, the eagle circled then headed east. Quanah knew what

Chief Quanah Parker and his family seated under the shade of a brush shelter. Such shelters protected them from the heat of the plains.

that meant. Fort Sill lay to the east. Quanah gave the messengers his answer. He promised that he would bring his people to Fort Sill.

Quanah came to the fort with 407 warriors. Their families waited on the plains. He would send for them if all went well. They arrived June 2, 1875. A crowd from other Comanche bands waited near the gate. Quanah at last came face to face with Colonel Mackenzie. Neither man showed his deep feelings. Quanah said quietly, "I have brought my people in. We will take up the white man's way." Mackenzie replied, "We are glad to see you."[2]

The Quahadi surrendered their weapons. They turned over their herd of 1,500 horses to the army. Then they set up their tipis in their new home. It was the end of the tribe's ancient way of life. Quanah later said proudly,

> I came into Fort Sill. No [one] ride me in or lead me by halter like cow. . . . I fought . . . Mackenzie. He warrior man, good soldier, but uses two thousand men, many wagons, horses, mules. Me, I had only 450 warriors, no supply train, ammunition and guns like him. I used this knife. . . . Mackenzie no catch me.[3]

The army did not treat Quanah harshly. He had killed and he had burned. He had done this to defend Comanche land. He had never sat down with white men. He had broken no treaties. The Army respected his bravery and his wisdom.

LIFE ON THE
COMANCHE RESERVATION

The Comanche reservation was on the edge of Fort Sill. The tribe had known this land for hundreds of years. It was rich with grass. Its many streams provided a sure water supply. Still Quanah's people were sad. No longer could they hunt for buffalo outside this square of land. Instead they drew their ration of beef and cornmeal once every two weeks. Sometimes the rations were delayed or spoiled. The Comanche often went hungry. From time to time the Indian Agent allowed the Comanche to pretend to hunt. Each warrior could choose a penned steer. When the steer was released, the warrior chased it on horseback. After the warrior shot the steer, the women butchered it on the spot.

The Comanche had never been farmers. They did not care to learn how to farm. The Indian Agent gave them sheep. They did not like the taste. They did not care to shear them and weave their wool. The Comanche just let them roam. Chief Mow-way mourned, "We are soaring eagles learning to live like barn owls."[1]

Indian Agent James Haworth helped Quanah learn more about his mother. He wrote a note that read, "This is the son of Cynthia Ann Parker. He is going to visit his mother's people. Please show him the road and help him as you can."[2] Silas Parker was Cynthia Ann's uncle. He lived in Texas. Quanah spent the summer of 1876 there. He visited his mother's grave, slept in her room, and learned some English. That fall he stayed on the Mexican ranch of Cynthia Ann's younger brother, John Parker. He had also been captured at Fort Parker, but by a different tribe. When John caught smallpox, the tribe had left him to die. He later married the Mexican slave girl who nursed him back to health.

The Comanche on the reservation lined up to draw their rations.

The Army allowed the Comanche to shoot their beef ration from horseback. In this way a brave could pretend he was still providing food by hunting.

One day, a bull chased Quanah across a corral. One of the bull's horns ripped into Quanah's thigh. John's wife bandaged the wound. Quanah said, "Worse than any hurt I got in battle. Bull worse than bluecoats."[3] When Quanah got back to Fort Sill, he drew his meat ration of six live cows. He had learned about brands from his uncle. He branded them with a *Q*. These few cows were the start of what over the years became a large herd. The tribe began to build its own herds.

On the reservation Quanah continued to lead his people. He sat as chief judge on the Court of Indian

Quanah revered the memory of his mother. He visited his white relatives and learned more of her life.

Offenses. There he mixed white man's law and Comanche law in reaching his verdicts. In one case, he decided in favor of the man with the greatest war honors. Some have criticized Quanah's actions. They say he sold out his people. They claim he became a white man's Indian. They accuse him of doing the bidding of the Bureau of Indian Affairs. Others say he was merely being practical.

In 1898, the United States went to war with Spain. Quanah urged the Comanche not to enlist. He explained, "My people quit fighting long ago. We have no desire to join anyone in war again."[4]

Quanah's leadership drew respect from the whites. Just south of the Red River, Texans named a town for him. A railroad, the Quanah, Acme, and Pacific, also carried his name. Quanah would spend 35 of his 65 years on the reservation. Though he traveled the white man's road, he always put his people first.

QUANAH BUILDS
COMANCHE PROSPERITY

Great herds of cattle roamed the South Plains. To get the beef to market, Texans had to drive their longhorn cattle north. The cattle trails to the Kansas railheads crossed Comanche land. Quanah charged the Texans one dollar per head. The tribe used the money to buy its own cattle.

When the railroad came to Texas, trail driving ended. Quanah knew the Comanche land was good for grazing. It covered more than three million acres. This was more than the tribe's cattle needed. Quanah leased the extra land to Texas cattle barons. One Texan, Dan Waggoner, leased 650,000 acres. The leases brought in from $30 to $50 for each Comanche.[1] But, the leases had to win approval from the government in Washington. Quanah went there to meet with the Commissioner of Indian Affairs. He also lobbied Congress on behalf of his tribe.

David Burnett was one Texan who became Quanah's

close friend. He built Quanah a large home near Fort Sill. The white house was two stories and had 12 rooms. A wide porch lined three sides. On the red roof the builders painted 22 large stars. That was more than any army general had. Over the years, Quanah had eight wives. He once had five at the same time. He fathered twenty-five children. Four of his wives lived with him in the Star House. An official told Quanah to choose one wife. He should tell the others to go away. Quanah said, "*You* tell them which one I keep."[2] The matter ended there.

In the late 1880s, Quanah and his father-in-law, Yellow Bear, visited Fort Worth, Texas. After a tiring evening, they returned to their hotel. Quanah did not turn off the gas. Instead, he blew out the light. In the morning, a maid found Yellow Bear dead. Quanah was unconscious. Despite the close call, Quanah recovered.

Whites flooded into the region when Cherokee lands were thrown open for settlement in the 1890s.

Quanah's house had more stars on its roof than any Army general wore on his shoulder straps.

As time went by whites wanted to settle on Comanche lands. They asked the government to break up the reservation. The October 1892 Jerome Agreement cut Comanche communal lands to half a million acres. Each Comanche was to receive 160 acres. They would share in a $2 million payment. The rest of the land would be open to white settlers. Quanah knew his tribe wasn't used to owning land privately. His Texan friends also wanted to keep the pastureland intact. Quanah went to Washington to argue against the agreement. He said the Comanche who signed it did not speak for the tribe. He claimed that translators had lied about the treaty's contents. His arguments influenced Congress. For ten years they did not approve the treaty. He also gained the tribe 480,000 acres more of communal land. In the end, however, the Comanche were stripped of thousands of acres of grazing land.

Quanah received many honors. He rode in Theodore Roosevelt's Inaugural Parade in 1905. Later the president came to hunt with Quanah in Comanche country. Over the years Quanah's band dwindled greatly. By the early 1900s, they numbered fewer than 1,200.

A few years later, Quanah fell ill with pneumonia. He sent for the tribal medicine man. The medicine man flapped his hands like the wings of the eagle. This messenger of the Great Spirit would carry Quanah's spirit to the Comanche afterworld. Quanah died on February 22, 1911. He was the last chief of the Comanche. After Quanah, no other held that title.

Quanah Parker and Biographer

Quanah was always willing to tell the story of his people. Many accounts of his life appeared in dime novels and books of western lore.

᭄NOTES BY CHAPTER᭄

Chapter 1

1. Weems, John Edward, *Death Song, The Last of the Indian Wars* (Garden City, N.Y.: Doubleday & Company, 1976), p. 186.

2. Brown, Dee, *Bury My Heart at Wounded Knee* (New York: Holt, Rinehart & Winston, 1970), p. 265.

3. Weems, pp. 193–194.

Chapter 2

1. Fehrenbach, T.R., *Comanches, The Destruction of a People* (London, England: Book Club Associates, 1975), p. 441.

Chapter 3

1. Lodge, Sally, *The Comanche* (Vero Beach, Fla.: Rourke Publications, 1992), p. 3.

2. Rollings, Willard H., *The Comanche* (New York: Chelsea House, 1989), pp. 23–24.

3. Fehrenbach, T.R., *Comanches, The Destruction of a People* (London: Book Club Associates, 1975), p. 128.

Chapter 4

1. Capps, Benjamin, *The Great Chiefs* (New York: Time-Life Books, 1975), p. 109.

2. Wilson, Clair, *Quanah Parker, Comanche Chief* (New York: Chelsea House, 1992), p. 67.

Chapter 5

1. Weems, John Edward, *Death Song, The Last of the Indian Wars* (Garden City, N.Y.: Doubleday & Company, 1976), pp. 151–152.

Chapter 6

1. Nye, Wilbur Sturtevant, *Plains Indians Raiders* (Norman: University of Oklahoma Press, 1968), p. 170.

2. Hilts, Len, *Quanah Parker* (San Diego, Calif.: Gulliver Books, Harcourt Brace Jovanovich, 1987), p. 114.

Chapter 7

1. Fehrenbach, T.R., *Comanches, The Destruction of a People* (London, England: Book Club Associates, 1975), p. 542.

2. Hilts, Len, *Quanah Parker* (San Diego, Calif.: Gulliver Books, Harcourt Brace Jovanovich, 1987), p. 119.

3. Wilson, Claire, *Quanah Parker, Comanche Chief* (New York: Chelsea House, 1992), p. 80.

Chapter 8

1. Hilts, Len, *Quanah Parker* (San Diego, Calif.: Gulliver Books, Harcourt Brace Jovanovich, 1987), p. 121.

2. Hilts, pp. 121–122.

3. Hilts, p. 123.

4. Capps, Benjamin, *The Great Chiefs* (New York: Time-Life Books, 1975), p. 124.

Chapter 9

1. Capps, Benjamin, *The Great Chiefs* (New York: Time-Life Books, 1975), p. 119.

2. Capps, p. 124.

GLOSSARY

band—A subdivision of a tribe, sometimes only a few dozen in number.

chief—A leader of a band or tribe. Often a chief was limited to a specific role, such as leadership in war or as a peace chief.

council—A meeting of the adult males in a tribe. All had the right to express their opinions.

Comanchería—The homeland of the Comanche; it included parts of Texas, Oklahoma, New Mexico, Kansas, and Colorado.

lodge—The Comanche's home. It was made of buffalo hides stretched over many poles.

medicine man—A Native American priest. Medicine men often combined foretelling the future with practicing medicine.

reservation—An area set aside by the federal government to be the permanent home of a group of Native Americans.

scouts—Skilled frontiersmen. Scouts served as lookouts, read tracks, found trails, and located game.

Staked Plains—A vast expanse of grasslands in western Texas and eastern New Mexico. It was called *Llano Estacado* in Spanish.

Sun Dance—A Native American ceremony held in the spring. During the dance the dancers suffered pain as a way of ensuring the blessing of the Great Spirit in the coming year.

treaty—An agreement between two governments. Treaties between Native Americans and whites often dealt with the sale of land.

tribe—A large group of Native Americans who speak a common

language, live in the same area, and have a common social organization.

troopers—Another name for mounted soldiers or cavalry.

vision quest—During vision quests, young Comanche men deprived themselves of sleep and food. When exhausted, they fell into a trance. They believed that the spirits spoke to them during these trances.

warrior—An adult Native American fighting man.

MORE GOOD READING ABOUT
≈≈≈QUANAH PARKER≈≈≈

Brown, Dee. *Bury My Heart at Wounded Knee*. New York: Holt, Rinehart & Winston, 1970.

Capps, Benjamin. *The Great Chiefs*. New York: Time-Life Books, 1975.

Fehrenbach, T. R. *Comanches, The Destruction of a People*. London: Book Club Associates, 1975.

Hilts, Len. *Quanah Parker*. San Diego, Calif.: Gulliver Books, Harcourt Brace Jovanovich, 1987.

Lodge, Sally. *The Comanche*. Vero Beach, Fla.: Rourke Publications, 1992.

Nye, Wilbur Sturtevant. *Plains Indian Raiders*. Norman: University of Oklahoma Press, 1968.

Rollings, Willard H. *The Comanche*. New York: Chelsea House, 1989.

Weems, John Edward. *Death Song, The Last of the Indian Wars*. Garden City, N.Y.: Doubleday & Company, 1976.

Wilson, Claire. *Quanah Parker, Comanche Chief*. New York: Chelsea House, 1992.

INDEX